Reading Charlotte Pence's breakthrough book, *Code*, I remember T. S. Eliot reminding us that humankind cannot bear very much reality. Perhaps the best way to bear the reality of our genetic structure, the code of her title, the thing that determines who we are, is to make poetry of it. After all, we want to believe that we have the free will to exist, to live and to love, and to celebrate our lives with our art. Charlotte Pence with her moving story of birth and loss has enhanced the language of poetry with the discourse of science, with the language of data. Her poetry reminds us that even as we know more and more about who we really are, life itself remains beautifully mysterious.

—Mark Jarman, author of *The Heronry*

Charlotte Pence's *Code* is deeply grounded in domestic settings that open onto broader vistas and "time longer than any dream." For Pence, motherhood holds the mysteries of the natural and human-made worlds—one where "we all began in dark and stars" but where we also wish "for sleep, / for peace, for the coming day to be better." For this poet, the maternal body and the body politic are closely connected, and *Code* is rich with urgent lines that pay close attention to the complicities of privilege and the need to shape the next generation's social conscience. Through a voice both tender and bracingly honest, Pence reinvents domestic tableaux in poems that are provocative, humane, and deeply necessary.

—Jane Satterfield, author of *Apocalypse Mix*

With *Code*, Charlotte Pence attunes both eye and ear, moving from a body in the contemporary urban to drawings on the walls of a cave in Spain. *Code* traces the death of so many--from strangers to the familiar and intimate: Evelyn McHale of the iconic Empire State Building suicide photograph, a grandfather, the poet Shira Shaiman. As Pence sequences the aftermath of loss in a chord of poems and personal essays, she also embeds Shaiman's own poems, honoring her late friend. This willful collaboration with the words of one no longer in the realm of the living results in a braiding of grief: each piece mourns for someone lost while also documenting what goes on in and around the mortal body. At its nexus, *Code* contains a narrative featuring the voices of a father, a mother who is dying from an inherited disease, and the mother's own DNA (in a prescient turn of poetic adroitness). Never have I encountered such tenderness and scrutiny in the scientific turned elegiac. Each of us originate from unique strands of genetic code, a code "beginning what is and has always been the same story, / but with different names for different animals." Pence is capacious in her attention to life, calling on us to witness what tinkers above and below surfaces, to carry on the legacies of those lost to us.

—Diana Khoi Nguyen, author of *Ghost of,*
a National Book Award finalist

CODE

CHARLOTTE PENCE

Black
Lawrence
Press

www.blacklawrence.com
Executive Editor: Diane Goettel
Book and Cover Design: Zoe Norvell

Copyright © Charlotte Pence 2020

ISBN: 978-1-62557-131-1

Published 2020 by Black Lawrence Press.

CODE

The word code *comes from the Latin* caudex, *the wooden pith of a tree on which scribes carved their writing. What, then, was the caudex of heredity? What was being transcribed, and how?*

—From Siddhartha Mukherjee's *The Gene: An Intimate History*

Dedicated To Shira Shaiman
April 1, 1971-February 24, 2014

Table of Contents

I.

The genome is only a mirror for the breadth or narrowness of human imagination.

—From Siddhartha Mukherjee's *The Gene: An Intimate History*

Orderly

For weeks, his button. Weeks later,
his button. Left on the bureau.
Dust squirming into its four eyes.
Like every annoyance, in the end,

if there ever is an end, his grew.
His mother was of sound mind.
Not body. He couldn't arrive in time.
The phone call came during a walk.

His dog pulled on the dark innards
of a flattened bird, wet with rot.
The quiet of chewing caught
his attention. Returning home,
keys still needed hanging. His coat.

Leash. The button—expressionless.
Somewhere, his mother. Of all the ways
to go, laughing is never one of them.
A stranger will cover her. Some nurse.

Some orderly. Is that what they're called?
Orderlies? Meanwhile, her body, her
bone house. Unbuttoned. Buttoned up.

The Weight of the Sun

I like the 4 a.m. feedings best, tilting
the rocking chair back and forth
with my toes, observing how the invisible

lines of our dark yard rest against
the lines of other yards—of other lives.
Before the sun rises, this small wedge

of the world momentarily in agreement:
everyone on this block wishing for sleep,
for peace, for the coming day to be better

than the last. I like thinking how the grass
growing a thousandth of an inch every
fifteen minutes is celebrating something

as I celebrate solving small mysteries
like learning a red fox is the one who
flattens the path through the lawn.

Mainly I like pretending I am the only one
awake, the only one seeing the world
at this instant. The navy sky, thick as blood,

is my blood, as the fracture of stars, bright
as raw bone, is my bone. I like being
reminded that we all began in dark and stars,

that the carbon, nitrogen, and oxygen
in our bodies was created 4.5 billion
years ago in another generation of stars,

that somehow if we could weigh the sun,
all rising 418 nonillion pounds of it,
we'd see that strength is never needed

to begin the day. No, it's something else.
Behind every square of light flipped on,
someone is standing or slouching,

stretching or sighing, covering
or uncovering her face. Someone
is thinking, *Today, I will I will I will...*

Attractions

Out of thirty-some jumpers off the Empire State, one
is known as "The Most Beautiful Suicide." Evelyn McHale.
There are photos, blogs, paintings. We can appreciate

the desire to imagine death as she portrays it. A swirling
white scarf with the ferocity of teeth. The sudden bang.
Position of deep sleep. She was one of the few ever to land

whole. After ending an engagement, she decided to leap big
toward nothing, avoiding all terraces and signage. Witnesses
commented on how far out she jumped. Seemed grateful

for that American go-for-it-ness. What's curious, though,
isn't the limousine hood that crumpled around her
like a black satin pillow, nor her crossed ankles, her gloved

fingers touching her pearl necklace, but on that day,
she, like the rest of us, dressed for the cold: buttoned
her coat, knotted her scarf, and covered her head.

While Reading About Semiotics

The cottonmouth charged, cleaving creek-side grass
with its wet-black, whip-thick body. Not in an "S,"
but more like a furious scribble, the snake thrashed
toward me with its wide ghost of throat.

I had often dreamt of snakes—coiling, hissing,
writhing—and woke sweat-damp wondering what it all
meant. Now, the keeled-scaled viper lunged and missed,
pursuing me as a dog would chase a ball.

I smiled, not at the snake, but at how the day
had suddenly filled with certainty. No question
over signifier and signified. No debate of snake
as it honed in on my soft skin. And the why:

a meal of rock bass I had unknowingly sat
beside on the bank, grey-black and deadly flat.

To Muck and Muck and Muck

Here I am again, seeking
something from another country.
Transformation, aren't you
a fist-sized bird? All claws
and low-yield clutches. You,
this stew of overused
Ganges, where we ride in a boat,
watch bodies burn on shore.
Last to go is the rib cage.
Belief dictates everyone cremated
on this sacred shore goes
to heaven, whatever the sin.
No wonder air is thick
with ash and grief. Floating
candles in bamboo cradles
outrun our boat, bob down
this holy, septic river
long emptied of oxygen,
toxic to touch. A mother dips
her hand into the waste. *Drink,
my love, drink*, she demands
of her child, limp on her lap.

Touring *Cueva de las Monedas* I.

Caves are not caves; they are thresholds
into other worlds. We enter, blink into being,
inhale as our ancestors would have for ripeness
of bear or carnage from cougar's feeding.

Safe scents of cold clay, mud puddles,
and prayer pull us in past stalactites,
past crystal-calcium horns, past
claw marks that rib walls in white.

The map-less dark reminds of centuries
when people knew they did not possess
dominion over nature and its predators, pathogens,
and meteors. Now we pretend otherwise,

claim bright futures begin with plans
and paths we clear with fire and hungry hands.

Sometimes, When a Child Smiles

mouth open wide and greedy, even the molars exposed,
it reminds me of a single afternoon when I'm passing

through an orphanage in Ecuador, distancing myself
with one-armed hugs and toy store gifts. I tour

cafeteria-sized bedrooms guarded by bougainvillea
scratching at windows, frowning palms standing shoulder

to shoulder. Outside the girls' windows, under the garden's
uncut hair rested a secret everyone knew and no one believed.

And I know the rules: I should not repeat it, should resist
telling a story about orphans. Yet how can I ignore it when

the sun angles from the west at five o'clock in May, when
light's neither new nor old, the color of freshly-squeezed lemons,

and it slices across a child's face at that silent moment
between grin and laughter when the open smile reminds me

of the girl who led me through the garden to where she found
the baby. But that's too common for a story. It is this:

For two months, the six-year-olds hid the newborn.
They snuck cartons of milk under their navy cardigans

and let the baby suckle off their fingertips. One girl chewed
her food and spit it inside the baby's mouth like she'd seen

stray dogs feed their pups. They named her Caramela,
a candy they wanted, and made her so content, the nuns

never heard her cry. Sometimes, when a child smiles,
I have to look away, for I know I could not do what

those girls did: accept a secret without fearing it;
spit into a child's mouth and know this, too, is love.

Among the Yellows

My grandfather died
        from slicing a hive in half.
A nest hidden in a log.
        His blade thinned to a dead-
end. What followed:
        a blur of bees. A man
running wild. Arms
        twice as thick as normal.
Neck vibrating out
        to in. He died before
my birth, which is why
        I imagine this:
a hundred split hexagons,
        shining, licked gold,
stirring with eggs, drips,
        pollen-dusted legs.
Yellow slits, like lit
        apartment windows
when darkness first peeks.
        Inside, strangers stirring
about their lives. Who hasn't
        peered in past politeness,
hoping to see—what is
        it exactly? Clicks and hums
humans make shaping
        their lives into order? The circles
to scrub skillets. Figure-
        eights to rinse toddlers'
hands. The curve to read
        the news. Shapes and slices
of the living. Obligations

of the alive.
I've stood outside
looking in, hoping
for something—
Once I saw it.
A slumped stranger suddenly
leapt from his chair, mouth
open, arms outstretched
to catch something
he loved. He uncoiled
his once crunched body
into a flow of honeyed fear
to reach beyond us both.
To hold, to clutch, to brush
off whatever mark was made.
I do not know what
to name the hived hum
that keeps us going.
All I know is
my grandfather's last act
was running. The bees'
last act was stinging.
And whatever was falling
in that apartment—
its last act was flying.

Joy Is Earned

—For Shira Shaiman, 1971–2014

It's easy to forget birth and death
are partners, hovering in a corner
at an otherwise pleasant party.
Right after the arrival of her second
child, the doctor said, It's
back: the cancer. My friend writes

the update now, subject heading
something with the word "joy."
The message lists the baby's weight,
his height, his favorite song—facts strung
along like blue and white pennants.
She tells us, too, that doctors agree:

no more options exist. I read the mass
email in my office, desk lumped
with half-assed student essays, bowl
of Dum Dums, quorum of hand sanitizers.
What is it that I had been worrying about?
We treat these bodies like rented

ponies. Wash them for the big events,
tie pink ribbons in manes,
then load them down again, ignore
them until everything slows to a stop
in a circle of circles. My friend
continues with what she wishes for,

wishing as if such a thing were possible,
as if a birthday cake were being carried
from the kitchen, the rest of us searching
for the light switch and the right pitch.

She leans in, candles casting a yellow
circle onto her face. *It's peaceful*, she says.

In my twenties, I worried about what I wanted
to be. Now I know. I want to be old.

II.

Love and death hold a standing invitation to any human home. So why is it that we greet them with surprise?

—From Adam Prince's "Eulogy for Steve Prince"

Codicil: An Essay
October 2017

Just last week I swam in the Gulf of Mexico and wondered if I'd ever need a coat again. I'd just moved to the port city of Mobile, Alabama. I was in the last week of editing this book of poems, so I was feeling something akin to a combination of relief and grief.

Then, there came an October chill. I had to take down the winter clothes after all. The boxes had taken a beating from the move. They were soft with use and crushed in the corners. One box looked particularly sad, particularly caved in. I don't know if it had been unpacked and dragged from all my moves since I left Boston years ago at the end of my MFA. Or maybe it was just the result of a manic packing job of mismatched items. Whatever the case, out came a visit from another time and place: Shira Shaiman's thesis from our two years together at Emerson College.

I don't remember her giving it to me. I had never even read it as a whole, although I had helped her revise many of the poems, just as she had helped me. And now here I was holding these poems amid my scarves, sweaters, and hats—cottoned leaf-litter on my hardwood floor. It was only appropriate that Shira would gift me her poems among the winter clothes. She was always teasing me to buy warmer clothes—and always right that I needed them.

Her thesis of poetry is titled *The Last House*, a reference I'm guessing she made to the history of the word "body," from Old English's bânhûsm, which translates literally to bone-house. Many of the poems are about the grief of her mother's passing—and some hint at her own fears for dying young as her mother did. They are eerie in their prescience. Although she wanted to publish her work, she never could bring herself to submitting, preferring to leave them safe within her circle of friends.

These past three years have been a series of swift-footed losses of wonderful people in my life: Shira, my father-in-law, and friends' sixteen-year-old daughter. Like so many strong emotions, grief is disorienting. I'm not sure of the appropriate action that can resolve such pain. I fear what tugs at the edges of what I'm writing: that resolution does not exist. I also fear the double-edged comfort time gives: an erosion. A distance from the moments the living once shared with the dead.

Although I thought my poetry collection had come to some kind of resolution, my friend Shira came around to remind me otherwise. I have no answers in this stay against oblivion, but I feel compelled to include some of Shira's poems. I have received permission from her husband David Pruskin to do so, and I have denoted her authorship under the poem's titles. Perhaps I happened upon a way Shira and I could hang out in the future: a book with both of our poems.

I'll end here with what Shira wrote in the abstract to *The Last House*: "Ultimately, active grieving is a potent catalyst for burning through to new layers of insight and knowledge, a new orientation of the self and the world. We grieve because we love and because we are loved."

Cell

—Written by Shira Shaiman

At first there was just one of you
sputtering, impetuous,
narcissistic, arrogant,
procreating
like mad
in my mother's marrow,
crazed as a rabid dog,
afraid to mature,
and having an identity crisis.
Cell, you seem
to have forgotten
your name, your address,
mission in life.
I should write it all for you
on a piece of paper
you could fold up,
keep in your wallet,
like my grandfather did
at the end of his life.
He had a kind of amnesia,
too, a confusion,
and we still loved him,
coaxed him to tell stories
about the War, the summer day
he met Ethel and fell
head over heels.
He kept her picture
in his wallet, too,
for 50 years,
not because he feared forgetting,

but for the regular pleasure
of remembering
the golden
face of his love.

Breathing Lessons*

—Written by Shira Shaiman

Last night I dreamed the disease
entered my body.
My head alabaster smooth,
I've become the face in the moon,
pasted in space and no ladder.
How will I get home, Mother?
How will we climb down?

*Note: This poem by Shira Shaiman is the second section of an eight-section poem
about her mother's illness.*

III. Code: A Sequence in Twenty-Three Parts

The word code, *I wrote before, comes from* caudex—*the pith of the tree that was used to scratch out early manuscripts. There is something evocative in the idea that the material used to write code gave rise to the word itself: form became function.... The genetic code had to be written into the material of DNA—just as intimately as scratches are etched into pith.*

—From Siddhartha Mukherjee's *The Gene: An Intimate History*

But sunlight was silent
streaming between trees.

I've failed you,
Mother's eyes seemed to say,

don't become like me.

—From Shira Shaiman's "Tender Break"

"DNA's Main Role is the Long-Term Storage of Information"

the geneticist writes. Then stops. *Very elegant,*
one of her lab workers said of the double helix.
The geneticist cannot help but think: Yes. DNA

is a whirl, a twist, a woman who will not have a seagull
crap on her shoulder as she accepts a glass of wedding
champagne. The drink tilted but never spilling.

She is a ladder no one can climb. A track laid for
a corporeal train. A hope to continue. What does
her voice sound like, she who is never done

talking? A bluebell in a field of red poppies?
Sand among sand? Or maybe her voice is one long "O"
as in: *Oh, I was hoping to see you again.*

A. and T. Meet

With all the pride of a yachtsman, I slid
my dinghy into the dock. She'd taken
to eating her sandwich on a bench along
BU's Sailing Pavilion, watching students sway
with the jib and boom. All chaos, but from where
I stood, the curved moons of the boats calmed.

I tied off the bow line, looked, then looked away.
A. kept looking, daring my long, short walk
toward her. "Water's choppy today," I said,
and eventually asked, "What do you do?"
"Geneticist," she told me. "I study the future."

I turned, squinting toward the water, warned
with white caps. "Aren't we all studying the future?"
"Worrying is not the same as studying," she replied.
The air wooled up cold and salty. She rewrapped

her winter-worn scarf, said she should get back
to work. "Why the hurry?" I asked. "There's time
in the future." And that's how it began:

me walking beside her before she realized that
despite how fast she went, I never meant to leave.

A.'s DNA Speaks at Child's Conception

Twisting around ourselves, we curl
at the center, copying hard, searching
and weaving for our dead mother's eyes.
They were hazel. Yet in her greenish-grey,

toasty-beige alternated with something wobbly.
A plain girl on a rusted green bike.
Tarnished spot on decaying leaf. Hesitation after
a compliment. *Very pretty,* Mother might offer.

Then, she'd clap once, ask, *What's next?*
as if to suggest life means never stopping.
After all the searching, we find the hazel rung
tangled among the bark-brown, yank it free

to the sound of a snap. Oh, we will see those eyes
again. Memory, we know better than to depend on you.

A., the New Mother, Wants More Instructions

> Sexual reproduction, as opposed to asexual reproduction, provides the greatest genetic diversity because the sperm and egg contain different combinations of genes from the parent organisms.
>
> —*From Field Museum, "Griffin Halls of Evolving Planet,"*
> *2006*

After her birth, two nurses switched the swinging
sacks of medicine: one clear drip for another,
an endless repetition. They say life is stringing
translations from a language with 4 letters: ATCG.

My too-thin baby is blooming bacteria in the black nest
of her shriveling cord. I am both mother and child, unsure
how to hold what they say is mine, how to coo sweetness
as other mothers do. We listen to the untying of my robe.

Do not misunderstand. I wanted this child, but *why* did
I want this child? Motherhood is obedience. The desire came
from some tangled place. A field folded over itself, littered
by old glaciers' lost pocket change of root and rock,

silt and salt. A field that burns clover and fescue
with the rabid hope of creating something new.

DNA Knows Once You Say It, You Can't Take It Back

"The human genome is a complex set of instructions, like a recipe book, directing our growth and development."

—From yourgenome.org

I. Cystic Fibrosis
Deletion of TTT on Exon 10:
ACTTCACTTCTAATGGTGATTATGGGAGAACTGGAGCCTTCA
GAGGGTAAAATTAAGCACAGTGGAAGAATTTCATTCTGTTCT
CAGTTTTCCTGGATTATGCCTGGCACCATTAAAGAAAATATCA
TCGGTGTTTCCTATGATGAATATAGATACAGAAGCGTCATCAA
AGCATGCCAACTAGAAGAG

II. Color Blindness

Cytosine to Adenine at 282
Thymine to Cytosine at 529
Thymine to Cytosine at 607
Guanine to Adenine at 989

1   ATGGCCCAGCAGTGGAGCCTCCAAAGGCTC
GCAGGCCGCCATCCGCAGGACAGCTATGAG
61 GACAGCACCCAGTCCAGCATCTTCACCTAC
ACCAACAGCAACTCCACCAGAGGCCCCTTC
121 GAAGGCCCGAATTACCACATCGCTCCCAGA
TGGGTGTACCACCTCACCAGTGTCTGGATG
181 ATCTTTGTGGTCATTGCATCCGTCTTCACA
AATGGGCTTGTGCTGGCGGCCACCATGAAG
241 TTCAAGAAGCTGCGCCACCCGCTGAACTGG
ATCCTGGTGAAACTGGCGGTCGCTGACCTG
301 GCAGAGACCGTCATCGCCAGCACTATCAGC

GTTGTGAACCAGGTCTATGGCTACTTCGTG
361 CTGGGCCACCCTATGTGTGTCCTGGAGGGC
TACACCGTCTCCCTGTGTGGGATCACAGGT
421 CTCTGGTCTCTGGCCATCATTTCCTGGGAG
AGATGGATGGTGGTCTGCAAGCCCTTTGGC
481 AATGTGAGATTTGATGCCAAGCTGGCCATC
GTGGGCATTGCCTTCTCCCGGATCTGGGCT
541 GCTGTGTGGACAGCCCCGCCCATCTTTGGT
TGGAGCAGGTACTGGCCCCACGGCCTGAAG
601 ACTTCACGCGGCCCAGACGTGTTCAGCGGC
AGCTCGTACCCCGGGGTGCAGTCTTACATG
661 ATTGTCCTCATGGTCACCTGCTGCATCACC
CCACTCAGCATCATCGTGCTCTGCTACCTC
721 CAAGTGTGGCTGGCCATCCGAGCGGTGGCA
AAGCAGCAGAAAGAGTCTGAATCCACCCAG
781 AAGGCAGAGAAGGAAGTGACGCGCATGGTG
GTGGTGATGGTCCTGGCATTCTGCTTCTGC
841 TGGGGACCATACGCCTTCTTCGCATGCTTT
GCTGCTGCCAACCCTGGCTACCCCTTCCAC
901 CCTTTGATGGCTGCCCTGCCGGCCTTCTTT
GCCAAAAGTGCCACTATCTACAACCCCGTT
961 ATCTATGTCTTTATGAACCGGCAGTTTCAA
AACTGCATCTTGCAGCTTTTCGGGAAGAAG
1021 GTTGACGATGGCTCTGAACTCTCCAGCGCC

III. Sickle Cell Anemia

Single Nucleotide Substitution (A to T) on Codon for Amino Acid
6:

CTGACTCCTGTGGAGAAGTCT

IV. Abnormal huntingtin (mHtt)

Short Arm of Chromosome 4 at position 16.3 features 36 to 120 CAG repeats:

AAACCG<u>CAGCAGCAGCAGCAGCAGCAGCAG</u>
<u>CAGCAGCAGCAGCAGCAGCAGCAGCAG</u>
<u>CAGCACAGCAGCAGCAGCAGCAGCAGCAG</u>
<u>CAGCAGCAGCAGCAGCAGCAGCAG</u>

A. Measures Her Child in the Hallway

> For the first time, researchers have managed to sequence
> proteins from the long-extinct [Tyrannosaurus Rex],
> leading them to the discovery that many of the molecules
> show a remarkable similarity to those of the humble
> chicken.
>
> —*From* The Guardian, *"Who Are You Calling Chicken?"*

Our preacher was mistaken. He said a miracle
had happened: a baby had been born.
But no. She keeps being born, growing
quarter-inch by quarter-inch: patella, pelvis,
tibia... Presents with mopped heads of ribbon
stopped arriving long ago. Yet this event keeps

happening. My own body keeps changing, too.
Tremors. Forgetfulness. They say to rest; take
this test. So, I urinate on command, tally
my fluid ounces, and tick off my snowy,
soda cracker appetite. This pushing onward, this

construction yard of cells, pulses a peaceful hum.
Yet it is not the peace religion promised. It's
better. Something misunderstood as fear.
It's what keeps us alive. What makes animals
run uphill before a flood. Kick the air.

And when need be, grab one another by the neck.
Twist a chicken's T-Rex throat. An end
beginning with a snap. Watch how that
miniature dinosaur will keep on walking.
The turtle, too, can swim without a head.

T. Leaves the Doctor's Office

When I think of all the ways we lie to ourselves,
I think of my childhood first. Old myths
I read after "lights out" in my triangular bedroom:
a converted attic, shiplap ceiling a pale, peeling yellow.

In books heavy as my fears, I read about earthquakes
caused by a large, twitchy catfish named Namazu;
I read of Neith, spider goddess spinning our destiny,
and of Divine Turtle, holding Earth on its back,

shifting to get more comfortable. I'd smile at
the stories, feel superior that I knew what to believe.
Today the doctor with his skull-white walls told us
how A. is really doing. It took four minutes.

Involved words we have been avoiding: fatal, genetic,
neurological. He continued with his checklist, his need
to "be clear:" rapid decay, severe personality changes,
unsteady gait, difficulty swallowing. Eight years max.

After the dispensing of facts, he encouraged us
to make another appointment. Shook our hands.
The assistant asked her string of blinking calls if
they could hold. I kept staring at the open scissors

on her desk, unusually large and ready to bite.
A. stood behind me, her face not unlike what I've seen
during fights: a preparedness to go down with the ship,
even if I were the ship. Today, I'm not the ship, but I will

be the one apologizing. I will soon begin what
friends will call a fight; a tough time; a senseless tragedy.
Beginning what is and has always been the same story,
but with different names for different animals.

What DNA Knows

What is death to us? We've heard that myth,
a ghost story to tell around a camp fire.
We're too busy to think. Our copies constantly

clamor around our waists like children. They rush
from their cramped classrooms into the red light
of the first time—wanting a push on the swings.

Surrounded by salty currents, how can we ask them
to stay close? They backstroke, flipstroke, frontstroke
toward the wide mouth of the deep where they break

into form. They mortar. They solder. They tower.
They make us proud. And what is birth to us?
Nothing and everything. We are one thing:

desire. Isn't that what all gods are?
More green, more grow, more grass.
We direct "circle time" every

second. *Criss-cross, apple-sauce*, we'll sing-song
to them, pointing to the picture book that instructs:
Initiation, Elongation, Termination. We know who

can sit together and who can't keep their hands
to themselves. So, we have an order: T and A.;
C and G. Our voice drones on and on,

a push, a pull, a parcel of wet letters to
the messenger who waits in the hall, ready
to run and weave, to repeat and repeat and repeat.

A. Experiments with Crispr on Herself

Running shoes: I wear them all   the time.
Run from home   to lab to home   to lab
and repeat. *See Spot run*—Remember

those books Mother read   to me? Now I read
But Not the Hippopotamus!   Now   I repeat
pipetting, forward mode: preparation,

aspiration,   dispense,   purge,   home.

Always back   home   I sing   to her
Little Bunny Foo Foo, hopping through the forest,
scooping up the field mice, bopping them on
the head.   There will be no fairy   coming
to save .   I saved you in this lab.   Micro
scope view of you as two: sperm   and egg.
A "no" to the repeat repeatrepeat of this disease.

We found a "go" in you. Now I will save myself:

Preparation   aspiration,   dispense,   purge,

home. home. See Spot run. And down I   come,
with a flowing   white   lab   coat,   hands
gloved in blue   plastic.   A final snap around   wrist
to tightly fit.   The cocking of   my grey-green   gun.

T. Cleans Out the Closet

Why do we keep the baby shoes?
Red Converse sneakers. White toes.
They say it is a reminder of how
small they were, how they depended

on us. Or maybe the grass-tongued
green toe is to remind me how to love
when I'm stained by what I've lost.
On days like this--early October, sky

wide as a blue ship drifting home--
I can be lulled into hoping a season
of good days could exist. The shoes
remind me I'm still here

to care for her. Not when she is asking
for something, but when she is not.

DNA "is to": A Quiz

1. DNA : Living Organism ::
   a. Birds: horizon
   b. Instructions: IKEA bookshelf
   c. Sentences: novel

2. Nucleobases : Instructions ::
   a. Letters: words
   b. Pink pastry box: Bavarian crème doughnuts
   c. A mother's voice: "It will be okay. I promise."

3. ATCG : DNA ::
   a. La-la-la: song
   b. ABCs: Latin Alphabet
   c. Yellow: doubt

4. Ribosome : mRNA ::
   a. Pressure: glacial ice
   b. Summer sky: notebook paper
   c. Reader: recipe

5. Proteins : Body ::
   a. Bricks, wood, cement, and nails: house
   b. Water: hydrogen and oxygen
   c. Dissatisfaction: a belief in satisfaction

6. DNA : RNA ::
   a. Dog bark: night
   b. Constitution: working law
   c. Hydrogen: oxygen

7. Metaphor : Truth ::
   a. Tongues: lies
   b. Antelopes: horns
   c. Comparisons: understanding

8. DNA : Story ::
   a. Fossils: story
   b. Cave art: story
   c. Bodies: story
   d. All the above

A. Waits for More Lab Results

My mother   told me   not to.
Be l ike her.   Sickly.   Unsatisfied.
When I was fifteen   sneaking out,
   easily   the screen would   push
away,   sounding like a muffledrum—
and then   I'd be standing,   still
as a stick   on the dew-lit grass.
One. blackened   form   against
another   blackened form:
brick block   of home,   stubborn
boxwood,   b lurred maple.   Our
edges   more pronounced   than
   centers.   I could   almost hear
thesleepingshell   of my mother's
   body   from inside the house
as Florida's   sand-white   streets
glowed around me, a n obstinate
g r I d.   Move,   I'd coax myself.
Return,   I imagined a parent saying.
Divide,   said the street corners.
Soon I'd walk to yet another turn,
another intersection.   Choice—
suggestive collar— left me to wander
all night   through   dayblind
warm weathered   mythic lawns
of youth, whose surrounding roads
were my mother's   softening bones.

T. Dresses Little U. for Her Birthday Party

Will Mommy be there?

I am trying to part this hair, this tangled spider thread. How can I part what refuses to be parted? It slurs like A's speech, a barbed-wire knot of will and ruin in my too-thick hands. Welling of red, of brakelight-burn on Storrow Drive, of stuck in the middle of mess, I throw down the comb. U. picks it up, and we hear her mother moan from the next room, a sound part beast, part babe.

Will Mommy be there?

I hold out the new party dress, flattened shape of girl without legs or arms, nothing flailing here, just crisp, obedient pink that moves how A. wishes her own body would, without thought or celebration. Our daughter will wear a smile too, and this new dress because I can't iron, and even when I do it looks like I didn't, and for once, for once, I want her to look as if A. had dressed her. I want our wrinkled world smooth as a sailboat on its tack. I want this day to be only simple tragedies: scraped-up knee, lost stuffie, dropped cake that falls blue-rose down. A star-shaped splat.

I want Mommy there.

And I want to find a matching white sock, one that is not grey-thin with use, one where the top doesn't droop, open to rain and dirt and some mom points it out, not with words, but with that thin-lipped, three-second pity-stare. What I want does not—

I want Mommy there!

Only Little U. has the patience to watch her mom walk down the hall. Once they tried to play Chutes and Ladders, but A's arms kept knocking the tokens from the board onto the floor. That floor.

A magnet at meal time. A.'s neck so twisted barely any food can go down it. Arms spasming, knocking the spoon from my hand. Little U.'s job is to wipe the floor and she never stops wiping and I never stop sing-songing: *Almost, almost*, while A.'s eyes flail and cross at her gruel and the spoon that refuses the mouth.

Will. Mommy. Be. There?!

Of course. Of course, I say. How can I part what refuses to be parted?

DNA Offers Some Palindromes on the Patent of CRISPR

Tumut, Akka, Catac, Hamamah:
all cities report the same news.
Tattarrattat
on my doors.
Did Eve refer
these thieves who alter what is not theirs?
Redivider
will take but not own the mistakes.

Was it a cat I saw?
Perhaps not a cat, but a trap.
Was it a bat I saw?
A trap is equal parts lure, pleasure, snap.
Was it a rat I saw?
A trap is deadliest when no one knows how to clear the snare.

At the Grocery Store, A. Stares at Packaged Chicken

Grey hum of the fridge
   Necks not a one
Chicken chorus chirps
     19 billion of us
Pale plucked puckered
3 for every person on the planet
No   heads
No feet
Nonetospeak
For its   glory
Its Reproductive Success
Open the bedside story of the best
       DNA
who cares not for quality
      of life
Success is   quantity
7-10 birds per square
      Meter
From TRex
   To jungle fowl
To lemonrubbed Sunday roast
Slanting a watery pink
  firm breast that bulges back
To the pricecheck touch
      (Bumble foot thrush
       Newcastle mushy chick)
Henpecked now the cook
DNA's fool   in the white cap
     Crowing *I Made This*
  "All natural"
       "In natural juices"

T. Writes a Letter to A.

Tonight, I took our daughter to Teddy Bear
Tumbling class. In the car, she worried nightfall
would hurt. I worried about the letter I can't finish.
Too many "you are," "you are," "you are…"

The letter too full of life, somersaults, round-offs
that begin with a two-footed gun shot off the floor.
The older gymnasts practice at the same time, impassive
as potted plants before flipping down the exercise floor,

stringing triple tucks, double layouts, side aerials.
Everyone expecting this miracle against gravity
to repeat. I can't decide if the quick raising of arms,
wrists clicking into attitude, chins up, is the right way

to end. I have to confess something. The best nights now
are those when neither of us sleeps, me rubbing your
shuddering back. It's our one power: creating another day
out of the darkness. Do you mind that I tell you what

the moon is doing each night? Waxing gibbous, first-quarter,
waxing crescent…. I don't know what else to say while I
clean the sheets under you, wipe the spittle from your cheek.
I can't say: *It will get better*. So, I describe the sky,

earth too complicated: waning crescent, three-quarter,
waning gibbous… Many different ways we describe
the moon: an old woman who never dies; a sister
to the sun; a hunter prowling for victims; a mother

playing with her star children while the sun naps.
The moon, though, the moon… Watch how she never
ceases. A woman forever hunting, forever singing, forever
watching the decline of something familiar beneath her.

DNA Cautions About Editing the Germline

We're just trying to repeat what's been. You
are trying to rewrite what might be.
It's like we're housed in the same high-rise,

but you live on the second floor while we look out
from the 23rd. We can see distance, both past
and future; you can only see what's dead

ahead. Don't be fooled into thinking you
understand this world. The flock of starlings
you point up to at evening's end, mumbling

the word *murmuration*, we look down upon.
We can see wind rippling their brown, satin heads.
We can see their obsidian eyes squinting against

their own speed. We can see their turning
by touching the tips of their neighbors' wings.
We are a lookout over this city and its moats

of grass among beloved parking lots where
cars line up like teeth in a zipper. Up here
in this bank of blue, this blink of clouds,

everyone is reduced to the hard roof
of their car. No faces, no throats,
no goals save one: keep going.

After the Last Prognosis

I own these woods where children play
their various games   of murder.
I can't relax   into   my grief.
It's full of thinning deer   bulging
ticks, children's screams outlining air.

Always the stitch of some dark bird.

Some of the best hiders believe
they'll never be   found.
                              Watch the red
sneaker without the leg.
                              Smell leaves
at their moment of   disarray.
Feel the sweat slip out from tensed pores.

All my life I've looked for light this slow.

Inevitably, the chillthrill
of finger tips chasinggrazing,
a hand swipingtheback. And then
is that   glee—or relief?—
in the v oice that declares:
                              Gotcha!

Olly, olly, oxen. Free free
free. Ollyolly Oxen free.

A's DNA Attempts to Console

We cannot offer wisdom about Charon's leaky
row boat cajoling you, swaying between
the worlds, but we can offer that the wooden floor

is always wet. Boards soft with salt and slosh.
Paint rubbed off by tapping boots. We can offer
that wisdom carries with it blood—despite

attempts to pretend that life doesn't require
the taking of life. That chimps don't plot
their victims' dismemberments. We cannot offer

old stories of the world beginning in a wink
of white or on the back of the sea
turtle. We do know how everywhere you go, you

are reminded of time. Of what has come before;
the albatross, white as sin, circling your head.
Everywhere birds—from wharfs to sky rises—

twill the air with song, and still you ask for more
song. We can offer that this thing called heat is fire
that seeks solitude: black stubble instead of field.

We can offer that matter trying to tear us apart
is neither dark nor invisible. That the words
"come back" are often the last you'll hear.

T. Takes Little U. to Her First Day of Kindergarten

Her red and white uniform peeks out
from a backpack wide as her shoulders.
Cars hem and hum as the crossing guard
bleats his whistle. The building greets

with its wide, rectangular mouth.
The older kids remind me to smile as
their loose bodies helix from one hello
to another down the hall. Each child

is last year and this coming one, everyone
momentarily tucked and combed, belted
and bowed, laces knotted with fresh
rhymes of "bunny goes into the hole."

But the kindergartners can barely move
their legs of knees and bruises.
My daughter has set her face on "don't
cry" with such focus it trips her feet.

She recites what's in her lunch:
water, carrots, cookies with dots like stars...
and finds her seat without looking back,
without saying goodbye, leaving me

mast-stiff among short desks
and sympathy-smiling moms, unsure
where to go. Then I remember the truth.
We said goodbye a long time ago,

the way it always happens when we
don't realize it's happening: three years

in the past, Saturday morning clutch
in bed, one of the last hugs when A's body

didn't jerk us away. Or maybe we started
our goodbyes when she was born, emerged
as her own person. I sat behind A. on the bed
as she leaned against me like a chair.

Suddenly, the awkward weight of something
light and hot and ours to wrap into a bundle
was with us, everyone united on the mattress
where fears and sweat collect. A. held a piece

of herself, and at last I knew what to do. I let go
as my wife held our child, our healthy child.

A. Listens to the Evening

No tears tiredness
        Snowflakes'
                dull thorns
pin me
    still as the white

Last snow   My body
        has shoveled it away

All the good things in this world—

Dusk calls them home

        A bright dusk
      A child's hands busy
with puzzle pieces

Clop-clop wooden shapes

shut tight Click-click—
                her teeth
                small squares
   emerge into   smile
pierce me
      into place

        into rest

Lack of want is beautiful

as a woman's hands slapping
        damp loaf of dough
                Shaping it all
into pale
        logs and tidy hills

Echoes of shapes my daughter lists now

rectangle   circle   square
            Clopclop   Clickclick

My child.
        Our eyes

DNA Speaks to Little U.

Quick as a cut, nightfall
came to the afternoon
where we sat on the nursery
floor when you were a baby.
White raft of a blanket
under us all. Suddenly,
a rustle, a whir, like the wind's
best dress. You squinted
toward the window,
trying to make sense of
the sudden jumps in light,
the soft thuds of cushioned
slaps. A clump of fifty
starlings murmuring
from one window to the next,
blocking and unblocking
light, beading and unbeading
their eyes, staring in at us
staring out at them.
At any moment, the darkness
could misdirect, bash
in the windows, but they
wouldn't do that. Would they?
We felt your soft form stiffen—
and we also stiffened, aware
for the first time that you
were aware. The birds, your
body, the abrupt turns of day
and night, everyone agreeing
and disagreeing on what
constitutes the thin ends
of a beating wing, the thin
ends of this thing we love: life.

T. at the Limits of the Possible

> "...At least one child had been lifted by an adult to produce
> some of [the cave art]. The process had been relatively
> complex as the adult had moved a distance of several
> yards while the child marked the surface of the ceiling.
> So, it was not a case of simply producing the drawings
> just anywhere... This all suggests that creators wanted to
> produce tracings at the limits of the possible."
>
> —Jean Clottes from *What is Paleolithic Art?:*
> *Cave Paintings and the Dawn of Human Creativity*

I read the caves are often conceived as female.
The art itself considered the oldest: 40,800
years. And I know we have to go, be a part
of something that lasts. "Help me pack?" I ask her.

She drops a plastic dinosaur into her sneaker,
then trots away. I want to take her hand, pull her
into my lap, tell her again of Spain and the art
she'll see, caverns larger than any house, time

longer than any dream. I wish her mother were here
to see it. Grief, like art, continues to teach
the limits of the possible. I want to take her hand,
lead her through damp-dark to where a child

years ago was led by her father to mark
the cave. Handprints reveal an index finger
shorter than the middle, a fact divulging
the artist was a girl, barely older than mine.

I will take her hand and walk along the slipping
mud floor wet from the mountain's slow
weeping. "Up there," I will say, pulling her
onto my shoulders, her body plus mine making us

as tall as a crow's nest. *Up there*, he too
must have said, holding fire burning on bison
fat, holding shell of red ochre
mixed with cave water. *There?* she must have

asked, pointing to what was almost out
of reach. Something on the edge of something.
Here, she decides, poking the ceiling's moon milk,
that wet, soft carbonate sparkling like stars

under the forked flame. I start to sway; she steadies
her torso, begins singing *Here, here, here,* combing
her fingers through the ceiling's fur while I roll
and bow, circle round, her fingers now flutes,

now waves, now stone, now snow, all rolling
through glitter, time, and space. Here she has
been born. Here she will stay. A part of this clay,
this cave, this moonmilk, mountain, mother.

IV.

History repeats itself, in part because the genome repeats itself.

—From *The Gene: An Intimate History* by Siddhartha Mukherjee

Anonymous

—Written by Shira Shaiman

Anonymous German cells
are being flown across the Atlantic
in an Igloo container
a special envoy guards
like a soldier his weapon.
For a moment, there's no cancer—
this is espionage
and Dr. Flomenberg the agent
waiting for the eagle to land.

While the plane taxis to the gate,
my mother is busy documenting,
snapping pictures of my father
with a paper camera,
then she paints on lipstick,
pats her cheeks with powder,
and poses for him from the bed.

Soon, a quartet of doctors surrounds her,
smiling behind their masks,
asking if she's ready.
Her big brown eyes dart
from one hidden face
to the next. "Don't worry,"
my father teases her,
"tomorrow you'll crave beer and schnitzel."

She presses an envelope into
the transplant coordinator's hands.
"Make sure this gets to him,"

she whispers,
before falling into a sedative sleep.

Whir and click. Whir and click.
The sound of a 35-year-old
man's stem cells
dripping through an IV pump
and a yard of tubing
into the veins
of this 58-year-old
Ashkenazi woman.

Back in the international terminal,
the envoy hoists his satchel
onto his shoulder to board the plane.
I imagine that deep in his bag,
wedged between the pages of a novel,
lies a white envelope with the words
for my doctor in a half-cursive print.

Folded up inside that envelope,
on its way to a young man in Germany
we'll never meet, the last poem
my mother will ever write,
a love poem.

Summer in Dorothy's Garden

—Written by Shira Shaiman

It slips from a branch
and drops beside me,
a slim green middle
with no end or beginning,
slithers through the startled weeds
and disappears into a thicket.
Dorothy assures me
tree snakes are harmless;
In fact, she's delighted
by the unexpected visit.
What do you think
it means—, she whispers.
That snake was meant for you.
In the story, God curses
man and serpent equally;
One to fight the land,
the other to eat dust,
both exiled indefinitely.
Here, the grass is overgrown.
blackberries choke the rose;
ivy climbs the clapboards
into the living room windows.
My friend is ninety-two.
This summer she lay down
her trowel in deference
to nature. *Eden's right here*,
she says, picking a peony,
meaning not our lives
in these bodies,
but this garden by the sea,

where each year the earth
succumbs, dies,
and begins again.

Stubby Horses and Why We Paint Them: An Essay

What first impressed me was the size of the cave itself. I had been imagining a little den with some art, something a bear could have curved his back against for a nap. But these famous Spanish caves, the *Monte Castillo*, are labyrinths upon labyrinths with four main cavities. Two cavities are open to the public: *El Castillo* and *Las Monedas*, both of which we toured. Made up of about 20 damp caverns, *El Castillo* is a vast dimness, shimmering where our flashlights ricocheted off the calcite.

Our daughter, Esmé, was the only child there. In all honesty, it wasn't the best place for a five-year-old: chilly, slippery, and dark. Plus, the tour guide spoke quietly in Spanish that Esmé couldn't understand. She stayed silent, gripping my hand while we walked, then getting wiggly when we would stop to stare at the 37,000-year-old outline of a bison, horse, or deer. The words—*cola, lomo, piernas*—became a sort of litany as the guide pointed out the tail, the back, the legs of a creature we would have otherwise overlooked as a series of scratches.

* * *

For this particular trip, we began in the quiet coastal town of Las Comillas. All honey-hued and cobble-stoned, it provided both an easy backdrop to photos and an easy drive to the famous painted caves. The buildings in Las Comillas were three-story stucco structures with red clay tiled roofs and brown-spindled balconies with geraniums spilling over with their insistent reds and fuchsias. It was beautiful. And whenever I'm somewhere beautiful, I am dead determined to rise to its challenge: to relax, to enjoy, to be happy.

In one photo, we were all smiling on a street corner, the town sleeping behind us. No cars on the road. No one else on the sidewalk. It was siesta time, which, despite our best efforts, was annoying us;

we had just arrived and wanted to see beyond the *"Cerrado"* shop signs. The date was September 28, 2016. My husband's father, his best friend and the one holding so much together, would die on October 9th. Soon after, my husband would lose his job. Soon after that, we would start marital counseling as we groped for causes of our anxiety.

In the picture, I see how the light was fading behind us, hitting a stone wall like a punch between the eyes. We couldn't find a place open for dinner that night until nine. And we were hungry at four. We ended up buying a baguette, some harsh cider, manchego cheese, and chorizo from the only open store. We brought the meal back to our rented weekend apartment equipped with dull knives and mismatched glasses. There's a picture of the dinner, with us smiling of course. Our daughter had recently gashed her forehead from dancing with pajamas on her head, so the wound—smack between her eyes—was an awkward peace-sign scab as large as a quarter.

I know the pictures only capture a few minutes of our five days there in Spain. Yet, over time, pictures, like stories, serve as both erasure and preservation. What's not told as anecdote or viewed in snapshot begins to fade. These two photos in particular now seem more like attempts to shape the future than they were attempts to capture the present. I wanted to tell my future self that we were happy.

* * *

About halfway through the first cave, halfway through more parts of a whole, more *cola, lomo, piernas,* we came across the famous image of a small hand outlined in brick-red. Archeologists speculate that these handprints are created by scraping the rock clean, placing the hand on the surface, and then dipping a hollow bird bone into a paint container such as a sea shell. The artist would then blow the paint over his/her hand, creating the outline in a very early version of spray paint.

It was the only child's hand in all the cave, our guide continued, speculating as to why the art even exists: shamanism, emergence of symbolic thought, hopeful communication to someone else...

"Mama," Esmé said, "I know why the kid did that."

"Why Esmé?" I asked, leaning in, expecting to hear something magical, something wise, something that no scientist—

"Because he was sooooo bored to be here."

* * *

In all the beach pictures from that weekend, the sky is a witch-hair grey swirled with stringy clouds. We are the only ones on the beach and having a wonderful time knowing no one can see our sand throwing, wave-kicking, hole-digging to China. It's just Esmé and me. Adam had to work—and take a break from so much togetherness. I don't think he phoned his dad during these five days. They had talked before we had left. His dad, Steve, had pancreatic cancer, but things were looking up. The last conversation was about the Dodgers and Christmas plans.

Still, Steve had had some surgery. And there was talk of possible complications as a result—blood clots for instance. I think now it was always on Adam's mind, but I didn't know that then.

* * *

On one scraped cave wall in *Las Monedas* stands the horse I keep thinking about. The wall itself is granite, streaked with amber-colored rock and cracked like a well-lived face. The horse itself is slanted so that his nose is the highest point on the drawing. Figures in these caves are rarely flat and centered like in photographs or museums. Instead, paintings follow the curve of the walls. Some are layered on top of one another. This horse is sideways.

He's an unremarkable horse, too thick in the belly, too rigid of mane, and detailed with only a thin line from ears to back. His feet are not hooves, but taper into points. Still, I love this stubby, pen-footed horse because here I saw it: how the wall was the horse. How the artist saw in the rock its rump and muscled neck and simply outlined that, calling out to a stranger to see what she saw almost

40,000 years ago. And the marvelous thing is that I saw it as have thousands of others navigating our own attempts to preserve what we have seen and felt. To pass a thought from one hand to the next as if it were a physical object, like a pebble.

*　*　*

On the beach munching on an apple gritty from sand, Esmé asked me something I couldn't answer. We were both cold and wet, but not ready to leave. Maybe she was stalling for time. She asked what made her "not me." What made her *her*. What made her a she with a gash in her forehead. And arms, she said, that will dig to China. "They will, Mom. They can dig all the way to the other side of the world. You don't believe me. But that's just because you don't know. You don't know anything."

*　*　*

For discovery, we first must uncover what we do not know. Scientists are now saying that even our understanding of the horse—that iconic image of power and freedom—has been inaccurate. Too male-centric. As it turns out, it is not the male horses, but the shorter, stubbier, ol' grey mares who are dominant, achieving their goals through cooperation, persistence, and bonds with others, both male and female. The reason we were wrong about the horse is because we had been studying what we created: the race horse or the work horse. Studies of wild horses in Spain and the United States are telling us what horses were like before we shaped them in our image.

This painting of the horse that I love is rarely mentioned in books. There are other more celebrated depictions of horses like the Panel of the Chinese Horses from Lascaux and the famous "Vogelherd Horse" after the German cave where it was found. This two-inch bit of mammoth ivory has attracted millions since an artist carved the stallion 35,000 years ago. Looking at pictures of this smooth stallion with his muscular, half-moon curved neck and his muzzle cast downward as if he's getting ready to bolt, I can understand why people love him. He was carved by someone who knew horses, who spent hours studying horses in the wild. Who knew a life that we do not know.

*　*　*

We love to create. To draw or write or sculpt. I've often wondered why researchers spend time theorizing as to why. To me, the answer feels simple. Isn't that just what makes us, us?

One of the first theories proposed about why cave art exists is the "art for art's sake" argument; Homo sapiens doodle to while away the time. But since the 19th century, that idea has fallen out of favor partly because of the skill of the cave art and partly because of its placement. Often, the art is placed so high as to need a scaffold or so far within a teeny cavern as to only allow room for one person: the artist.

The other theory is that the art is part of a ritual, maybe a religious ceremony that also involves hallucinogens.

But in one way or another, whatever the theory, isn't it all a stay against oblivion? Photographs, words, graffiti, stories, cave scratches of a horse plump in the middle and short in the leg?

To me, it's a reflex, like breathing, eating, sneezing, loving. I cannot stop any of these as I cannot stop trying to take what is in my head and present it again, through these symbols we call the alphabet. To pass a private thought to another's mind. It is what I desire to give—and to receive—just as someone would proffer a plate of food before opening the wine. A platter of offerings, of thoughts, of memories. Of *cola, lomo, piernas.*

*　*　*

Laura Lagos and Felipe Barcena at the University of Santiago de Compostela in Spain are two of the scientists disrupting our ideas of horses. They study free-roaming horses called *Garranos* who live in the tough hills of northwestern Spain and northern Portugal. "It turns out that, unlike stallions, mares do not need to have huge fights to get what they want. Instead, they use the technique of persistence," Wendy Williams explains in her article on the subject at *Scientific American*. She recounts the story of one "plain-Jane mare with a sagging back and poor coat" who was named High Tail by researchers because "the dock of her tail sat a bit too high on her croup."

High Tail's story is one of a love triangle, which involves her longtime buddy and mate Sam and another male, Sitting Bull. Sam and High Tail first became friends in their youth and then struck out on their own, gathering other mares in a peaceful co-existence. Peaceful, that is, until Sitting Bull, the younger stallion, started sniffing around, trying to mate with High Tail and the other mares in their group. Sam was continually fighting him off, but Sitting Bull was employing persistence as well as power; he marched along the perimeter of the group, studying them. Waiting for his chance. And his chance did indeed come, in the form of a flash flood.

*　*　*

Thinking about all of this—horses, art, memory—I couldn't shake Esmé's question from earlier in the day when we were playing on the beach: "What makes me alive? Me *me*. You *you*. Daddy *Daddy*." There are really three questions there: Why do I exist? How did I come to be this being that I conceive of as myself? And what makes me distinct from you?

I thought of her questions as I left the caves and walked alongside the mountain that guarded painting upon painting of hands, red dots, horses and more. Each painting is someone else's conception of a hand, a red dot, a horse. A conception somehow simultaneously distant and similar to my own.

In Jean Clottes's famous book *What is Paleolithic Art?*, he speculates on how there is not a universal definition for art itself, but ultimately, he says it is the "way in which humans distance themselves and reconstruct the world around them." While I had arrived at these caves hoping for connection to not just my family, but to another time, another world, another mentality, I ultimately found something more interesting: an attempt from one person to distance himself from others. To distance oneself from one's experiences is the first step to creating art. The next is an attempt to recreate something that is a blend of both: self and other; experience and imagined experience; past, present, and future.

*   *   *

Before any self can be created, one needs something basic: water. And that's what almost killed High Tail and her band who live in the Pryor Mountains where fresh water is a constant challenge. One day, they descended the craggy, steep walls of Bighorn Gorge to drink only to be greeted with a sudden flash flood. With the water up to the knees, they scrambled to get out, but rushing water cut off their path.

For two weeks they were stuck there in the water, slowly dying of hunger. Sitting Bull was also there, high on a ledge looking down at the weakening Sam.

When the horses finally made their slow, slipping, wet-walk back up, Sam had lost a lot of his muscle—and Sitting Bull jumped him. This time, it was over. Sam fought back but the bloody battle ended with Sam alive, but unable to rise. Sitting Bull, though, was all movement, cantering around the group to push them on and away from Sam, and lunging to bite High Tail whenever she so much as looked back at her companion since youth.

Repeatedly, she tried to leave the band to be with Sam, facing the teeth of Sitting Bull each and every time. She wouldn't allow herself to be bitten, though. She'd return and continue to look for an opportunity. Sure enough, one day when Sitting Bull wasn't paying attention, she flew off to find Sam.

And she did. The two of them roamed the plains together until he died in 2010, six years after they struck out alone. They had found that which we all seek—a connection. A willing partner. And they were not about to let each other fade from their vision.

*   *   *

Four days after returning from Spain, we learned that things had taken a sudden, unexpected turn for my father-in-law. A flash flood of bodily failures. My husband tried to make it back to see him again, but he passed away during my husband's flight. The last conversation on the phone with his father was an incoherent one, in which time and space rolled like the waters in the Bay of Biscay. It is a conversation that Adam will not recount or even summarize. Maybe he wants those words to be left where they are: in the air.

About a year after his father died, Adam asked for us to try EFT (Emotional Focused Therapy), which focuses on adult relationships and how to create positive attachment bonds. From our year in EFT, we have started to realize how we did not know how to be individuals *and* a couple. Both of us have different reasons for needing independence—no doubt partly influenced from the American myth of the individual; that lone figure striking off into the sunset with his horse, gun, and canteen.

Still, reaching toward another person and being vulnerable with your innermost thoughts is the real courageous journey. For my husband and me, to take our internal thoughts and make them known was tough—even though we did this in our writing all the time. Art was the safety, humans the risk. There are too many Sitting Bulls out there waiting for a moment of weakness.

Yet that desire to reach out remains as I saw again and again on the cave walls. At times, the drawings were layered on top of one another just as artists now will paint over a canvas to create again. We can't stop trying to communicate with others even if this means obliterating what came before. *Turn toward one another when you are angry or hurt*, our therapist keeps reminding us. *Not away.*

*   *   *

I left the caves thinking of that horse flank and saw in the field below a living horse—then another, and another. A cowbell echoed. A hawk screeched. Since I had been in the cave, the sunny day had turned hazy, and I walked now inside a cloud as a I made my way down to the parking lot, thinking about all the figures I had seen, including a five-pointed star—a shape that always gave me fits to draw in elementary school. An odd shape, really, as the stars don't really look like those perfect five points. But here we had the same shape with those five points being sketched 40,000 years ago.

As I walked back down, I also wondered about why there are rarely people in the cave art. It's estimated that only two percent of drawings are of the human form, and then they are merged with that of another animal, such as the famous drawing of a woman and bull, an image repeated years later in literature with Europa and the sacred bull.

I wonder if the reason is connected to the growth of art as individualistic expression versus communal recollection. Poetry has moved in that direction from the troubadour age to now. Where is the self in these very early examples of art? Why aren't there self-portraits on the cave walls? All we have are red hands without arms reaching out to the dark.

V.

Incidentally, there is no architect.

—From the *Selfish Gene* by Richard Dawkins

Lightening

You are dropping,
my baby. Twisting
your way down. Lightening,
they call this. Feeling
of levity. Certainty.
Lightening they call, too,
the moment before
death. Another release.
Such contrasts, yet
the word's origin
offers no explanation
for such a linguistic
hike. No old root
to mean: "light from
nightfall, nightfall
from light." With you
inside me, I walk
these brown woods
where deer thin
to vines, where old
men walk along ponds
hardened into milk-white
stones. What's to come?
The flickering
gait of a scared fox.
Fiddlehead fern unfolding.
Twice, the ground will call
at either side of your years.
Count them: the seconds
between flash and crack,
then divide by five
to learn the distance

between you, the storm,
its rains.

Love Between Parents

Once I gulped sex, unsure of its bounds.
      Now I read how scientists are unsure
            of computers' boundaries.

Outside, winter hardens into March.
Blood-dot head of the woodpecker
    needles.

            The essay theorizes
            Computers' limits are
            the mind's
            limits.

      My theory admits sex after a child
            is weird.

            Our bodies have become
      a rented text weary with underlines.

Love   is a square of white
        where once hung a picture.

      Memories of cravings—
      sleet-shined and treacherous as winter roads.

      We are
too close. Double pane windows dull
the brighter the sun shines.

            When I see my love
            at a distance,

      leaving a drugstore,

sliding glass doors stretching, too bright day,

long strides,
        I almost don't recognize him,

then do—that feeling
like a rush and being rushed,
one screen to next.

Always I wonder where is the end?

So, I turn to what is in front of me:
the window, dimpled with ghosts of rain.

Helen of Troy

The Trojans kept Helen for twelve
years, winning at least a little while.
So often we focus on the loss
rather than the years of attainment.
But any love that matters will one day
be taken for granted. Last night,
lying down to sleep next to you
on wrinkled sheets, warm where
the dog curled, cold by our feet,
I realized as your hand grazed my thigh
you hadn't touched me all day.
Each morning when I wake, I understand
you're an eagle scanning the next ridge.
The bed heaves as you rise first,
your steps hard, stiff, while the erupting
sky behind you eases from gravel gray
to blue. You don't glance back
at the soft curve of my body,
not yet rigid with the day's to-dos.
What you do is place cereal and fruit
in a bowl, then call my name.
The milk cold. The peach sliced.
Without motive or need,
we sleep, eat, read, breathe together,
you running a hand under my shirt
whenever you want. But I was talking
about Helen, about how she loved
as she wished at least once, willing
to witness the loss of a world for it.

A Pantoum from the Headline: "Y-Chromosomal Adam and Mitochondrial Eve Never Met"

You always suspected there was more to Adam and Eve,
and now you read they never met, lived apart,
like a contemporary cyber couple. Comfy in pajamas at desks,
connected but not connected, claiming a love never tested.

Couples who never meet live apart from the rest of us, remain
in prelapsarian puppy-love during an era of post-coital tristesse.
Connected but not connected, claiming a love never tested
by the rickshaw of kitchen cleaning or tock of biological clocks.

Oh, prelapsarian puppy-love does avoid post-coital tristesse,
for love is simpler when only molecular, allowing Eve to bypass
crowded rickshaws, kitchen cleanings, and her biological clock.
Time differs. Apples remain polished, unbitten,

for love is simpler. When only molecular, Eve bypasses everything
that makes humans human. Binds herself not to us, but atoms.
Time was different then. Apples remained apples. Red. Unbitten.
You always suspected that there was more to Eve than Adam.

Touring *Cueva de las Monedas* II.

We shine our flashlights on the rough rub
of charcoal strokes. What lingers
after 37,000 years is outlines of fingers,
rusty-red hands, deer, bison, bear cubs—
and far from the others, a plump colt,
aimed toward the cave's ceiling. Gaskin, hock,
and fetlock tread horizontally below the neck.
His muzzle nibbles rocky air as he floats

in a field without sky, grass, or Spanish gorse.
I reach out for this groundless world
to join the solitary animal slanted toward
a carbon future that will soon exist
without me or you. Only this slanted horse
and sliding rock, stationary even as they shift.

Black Silhouettes against a Pink Sunset

They move
more like darkness
than deer,

this trio
who nibbles
knee-high

bluegrass,
this trio
I mistook

as straight-backed,
head-bowed,
night

nipping the edges
of field and forest,
while the sunset

behind them
slices sky
a blinding pink.

This trio stops
and starts
and stops

along the same path
my family
of three

walk

"for air."
What is

air
but shared
possibility?

And what
is the name
for those

moments
when worry
feels distant

and tamed—
when we
return

to deer
to darkness
to certainty

that this coming night
is neither for
nor against us.

A Swim Stroke in Verse: Seventeen Giant Manta Rays and One Hut

Because the ocean steals
       the color red
              at certain depths. Because

the ocean steals.

Because the ocean—
a hundred feet of it,
is squatting on my back.

Because.

A gentle, ungentle casket.

I tell myself to breathe.

———

Past the depth for recreation. Past
the depth for seeing the surface. Past
the depth for assistance, if need be.

The nothing impressed. No fish, no speech,
no coral. Ocean's bottom like the beach
somewhere, some waves, above me.

A desert in the ocean. A cleaning station
for giant manta rays. A meeting of titans
and tiny wrasse who munch off parasites.

I'd been told to lie on the ocean floor
and wait. But the currents tumbled, tore
me over myself. I grabbed at sand, trying

to embed, to claw, to force knees down.
Legs kept lifting, pulling the body out. I found
a shell and spiked it. But it, too, failed to hold,

leaving me to thrash in an effort to stay.
Leaving me to suck more oxygen, stray
from the group, miss the first glint:

the ghost of a white fin.

———————

Let me draw a picture. I
was right there—at the top.
But they—creatures that live
in the deep—were deeper. I was at
the summit of an underwater cliff, if
you believe cliffs exist under water. The world
a mimicry of mountain ranges. Some groan under
water; some glare above it. But the same possibility exists:
to hang one's head over the edge, wonder what else is out there. They
are out there. I hoped they would glide up the cliff wall, glide over
my back, wait like I was waiting for the cleaner fish to come nibble
along their bellies. Parasites irresistible as a platter of wet grapes. Slime,
a wine. Like all travelers, I looked over the edge, into watered sky that
would squish my lungs, loop my brain, carbon my blood. And I felt tempted
to jump.

———————

Into the blue.
Into the blue, the divers call.
Into the blue, the divers call the depths

that will wring out

their lungs.

> I stared, wanting it.
> Wanting it to change.
> Wanting to change into it.
> Wanting to change into its color of silence.
>   Glide

into the blue that burns off the world,
off the problems of the body,

wanting to ride the thick,
                the thick neck of wind,
        of horse,
of February plains
when nothing
        is coming
                but more.
                (cold, wind, dark)

And then,
        out of this country,
out of the blue—
White.

White glint.

White glint not of a ghost

        but a giant.

———

Flash of flapped wing emerged
into another wing, a belly, a tail,
and then the rectangular,
car-wash mouth.

It swam low and close,
an arm's length away, watching
me watching it. I stared
at the eye,

moving slowly in its socket.
Stared at the body
the size of a living room.
What lured me

was the calm. He flapped
his wings, only once, in order
to hover, a stroke as a way
to stay in place.

Then another arrived, another,
until seventeen rays coasted by.
Beginning of one, ending
with another.

———

We all think of suddenly ceasing to be. Enjoy the nibble of it. Isn't
that invisibility what we are singing to as we drive fast and west
through red rock country? No one around except haze ghosting
the road. Or in the Midwest, the skittering rows of corn that flip by
like decked cards—and the one dead stalk stands like an open door
to somewhere grander. Or the X of wood over the old mine shaft.
Tempting. What is it, though, that calls us back? Dishes? Daugh-
ters? Anxious dogs looking out the front window? I imagined a hut
hunkered at the ecotone where beach becomes buried in palms.

A hut with a dirt floor. A woman is crouched on the floor with her arms over her head. Elbows make divots in the ground. She will stop crying once she can forget about herself, just for a second. Maybe she'll smell the damp clean of dirt, so close to her now, and will realize she needs to wipe her nose. The snot is tickling. And that thought leads her to notice her hair, also tickling, and she'll wipe the strands from her face, the universal gesture that means: I have decided to return. I've decided to return to the world as it is—the frustration, the sadness, the water that always needs boiling. She will begin again by clearing the table of its noodle-stuck, oil-slicked plates, washing them for the thousandth time. The air in the hut, the drone of the radio, the scratch of the lizard on the roof... And there is the chicken. Her favorite one. It needs her to throw out the feed again. She will scoop into the grain sack and toss the feed across the yard with such force. The yellow arc that hangs before the clatter is not gold, but that other thing we need even more.

Zwerp

Three mud-
puddle frogs

leap-flee
from me

four feet
up ahead

this dirt path,
leap-flee

into the ever-
present puddle

of possibility
that both dog

and I know
will wet his paws,

will muck my boots,
will tuck in dirt

dark with decay
and morning dew.

Three plops
pronounce fears

then disappear
under the swirl

of water stirred,
the sound similar

to the word "zwer"
hunters use

to describe partridges
taking flight

from beige brush.
These frogs

take light--
blur it, bold it--

with long, slick
legs, all muscle

memory
of place and space,

amphibious
with daily doubts,

suspicious
of my legs' scissoring

sureness, my dog's
nosy snuffleness.

Her snout, white
with age and air

of what we once
were. Now,

two souls
who know

a walk and warmth
can soften

jagged worries,
two souls

who peer into muck
hoping for bulge

of recalcitrant eye
from spy to spy,

but all that remains
is the wobbling

puddle, the smoldering
mud, the thought

that movement ahead
on the miry path

makes a sound
I name now

as "zwerp,"
a word suggesting

foot-fall
and leg-slap,

fear and safety
found, a word

that suggests
to leap, to flee,

for the covering quiver
of water's sleep.

How to Measure Distance

I. *Only Use Light Years When Talking to the General Public*

or to squirrels who test spring between two
branches. Or to a new mother saddened
by thoughts of earth and its death; sun's death;
her death. She watches her husband leave
the room for a burp cloth, wonders, could she
do it without him? What's the measurement
of distance between two people growing
too close, too quickly?

II. *The Measures We Use Depend on What We Are Measuring*

Distance between parents? Hills? Rogue comets?
Within our solar system, distance is
measured in Astronomical Units.
Or "A.U.," an abbreviation that
sounds similar to the "ow" of a toe
stub. Or similar to the sound of a mother
teaching the beginning of all sound. "Ah,
eh, ee, oo, uu." Watch her mouth widen,
purr, and close. This is the measurement
for what we call breath.

III. *For Most Everything Else—Stars, Galaxies, Etc.—the Distance
Unit Is the Parsec (pc). This Is a Convenient Unit*

for gathering groceries, grains in silos,
gasses we cannot package and discount.

*This is convenient, too, when measuring
stars' distances by triangulation.
1 pc = 3.26 light years =
about the distance to the nearest star.*

An equal sign leading to an "about."

An estimate. A close enough.

Close enough feels safer than being wrong.
Or exact. "Close enough," we say of that
asteroid skimming past our atmosphere's skin.
"Close enough," we say when he returns
with a guest towel.

IV. *For Distances Within our Galaxy or Other Galaxies, It Is
Kiloparsecs*

She is unsure what fatherhood will do
to him. Accurate measurements require
one to know where one stands, where one belongs,
where one is going. Rub the toe
of the blue shoe into the dust. See how
the dust is not a bit bluer. The shoe,
a bit browner. Distance = a thing
between and against.

V. *The Exception to These Units Is When One Is Studying a Smaller
Object*

Father to mother to early zygote.
Branch to squirrel to tail-twitch and release.
Knee to toe to spring mud too soft to flake.
No units for these.

VI. *One Might Say, "Its Radius Is 5 Solar Radii", Meaning It Is 5 Times
the Size of Our Sun*

Her fear is five times the size of sun, five
times the hours of sleep or lack thereof.
Five times the huddle of father, mother,

child. Five times the energy created
for one nap as opposed to the length
of that nap, that leap.

VII. *She Wants Answers*

but is realizing that won't happen.
She fears the truth that nothing stays the same.
Rashes fade, yet skin will prickle again.
Cries will quiet, yet the quiet will cry.
The man will leave, yet the same man will leave
again. That's why eyes are bloodshot, why she
answers questions as if she doesn't care.
All answers are "almost" or "about"—
everything moving. And this thing called light
years is a distance she can't comprehend.
Yet somewhere she squirms at one forever-
changing end of it.

Some Madness There

*"It's only fully modern humans who start this thing of
venturing out on the ocean where you don't see land. Part of
that is technology, of course; you have to have ships to do it.
But there is also, I like to say, some madness there."*

—Svante Paäbo from "The Madness Gene"

They must run, these soft creatures
we nurse and lullaby. Must wriggle
across the dog, up the shelves,
under the fence. It's not enough,

never far enough. They flock to where
ground softens into waves, into riptides.
There! they say, pointing to the imaginary
line where sky and sea meet. *There!*

they say to pocks on the moon. *There!*
to the dim disk of Mars. "Here"
is where they need to leave more than
"there" is where to go. Often they ask,

What will we find? Not as often do
they ask why they must flee
the known, the home, the family
who stands behind and waves.

That's one thing we're good for, we
families: It's our job to wave.

Mourning Chicago

I left the radio on too long,
and so she hears the morning news,
my five-year-old licking peanut butter off toast,
stops, holds it in midair, and asks, *Cops shot two kids?*
Will they shoot me? And I know how to answer but I don't know

how to answer. I know
that because she is white and I am
white and her dad is white, even our Toyota
is white and our dog a beer-shine blonde, the cops
will not shoot her. And I am relieved and sickened by my relief,

and so I say, I left the radio
on too long, but that is wrong, and so
I say that cops are people who make mistakes,
but I know it's not just the cops, but we who leave
the neighborhoods, the schools, the YMCAs, we who leave

the cops alone
to tend to what everyone wants
to pretend doesn't exist, be it poverty, paranoia,
the pointlessness of trying to improve when—Her dad
interrupts, says, Cops help us. I shake my head, say, we cannot

lie, although I lie
all the time, and he shakes
his head, suggesting she's young
enough for this lie, and I think how differently parents
across our Untied States hold these conversations in the kitchen,

everyone chewing on a different
snap, crackle, pop as they discuss what
to do when approached by a cop. And it's not just
because we're white, but also that we have enough money
to keep the tags up, the brake lights on, the accent with no "from."

My mom taught me
to say, Sorry Officer, I'm just
running late to Grandma's house, as if life
is a woodsy trek sometimes interrupted by a furry
wolf whose teeth can be appeased by a smile and a please.

I remove the fairytale
for my daughter, say they are
another "dispenser of violence in this world,"
and my husband says, Stop, and I say, I will when
it stops; he says it'll never stop, so we fumble for the volume

as the radio mumbles,
our daughter now equally confused
by the two: Why they killed kids and why they
will not kill her, so she asks again, *Why* won't *they shoot me*?
as the radio keeps up its monotone morning prattle to go down
with coffee and cream, its morning reporting: *Chicago, Chicago, Chicago.*

I'm Thinking Again of That Lone Boxer

practicing in Baltimore's Herring Run Park,
floating over the fogged field. City gridlock stood
beside him as he slipped and bobbed, countered
and angled, practicing the art of when to back

down, when to dodge, when to defend.
I'd just been thinking about all I'm losing
in this thing called motherhood
when he delivered a left hook that could've spun

that string of blue stars around anyone's head.
I refuse to say he was a dancer, for he was
what he always was: a man fighting in an empty
field against himself. Yet as long as I remember

that taut curve of back ready to uncoil a punch,
bow of head ready to receive a blow, how
can I not believe in the possibility of peace?

Grief

When the sky is morning-bright,
three men will arrive in a pick-up.
Roofing hatchets, pry bars, and lawn rake
will poke from the bed like steel flowers.
Only the foreman will speak to you while
the others hover at the curb. He'll tell you
his plans, speaking slowly, simply,
his voice deep as a hole in the ground.
You offer: "I hope it's not too hot
for this work today." And he will answer:
"Mind over matter." Or is it matter over
mind? No matter. Never mind. The ladder
will clink up, the roof shingles will smack down,
the plywood you've never seen will swing off,
dark with water and softness. The house is laid
bare to birds, the sun, the warming ozone,
to anyone bored enough to study the celled attic.
Once the work is done, you'll thank them
and go back inside. From the street, others will
not notice a change in the house; the roof grey
as before. Yet a new weight rests, so what
is to be done with this? The roof will mute
its thoughts, push away the sun, the rain, push
the squirrels back into the trees. And the walls
will do what they always do: crack without a sound,
refusing, refusing the mumbling ground.

If It Ever Leaves, Where Does It Go?

Eye-to-eye with water hemlock, red-winged
blackbirds, cattails' coffin-velvet shoots,
Captain Jacobs points out bumps in the water:
"gator snouts." In these hot months, the cold-
blooded dangle vertically in the Bay, seeking
out the chill six feet below. Exposed
noses become small moorings of salted
flowers, turtle meat. Their stillness startles,
as does their presence, although Mobile Bay
teems with them. Glancing toward my husband,
stiff with mourning, I realize I steer away
from speaking about his father as if that act
can propel the grieving into everyday living.
We navigate the boat out of tangled murk
toward the glassy scrim of calmer, deeper
water. Engine gurgles off. The wake's rush
slaps us silent. Then, a heron lifts. The boat lists
to port, starboard, back again. Below
the surface, chain-like necks, green-black scutes
in shapes of pendalogues, and ghost-white
bellies light this world. What hangs
in the water's harlequin haze sways with us.

Notes

A., The New Mother, Wants More Instructions

A, T, C, and G stand for adenine, thymine, cytosine, and guanine, which are the four nucleotides found in DNA that instruct the body on how to build itself. Sexual reproduction involves meiosis, which is the process of a cell doubling its DNA, shuffling its genes, and then dividing the shuffled DNA among four cells.

Thank you to the Field Museum for the permission to use the epigraph in this poem:
(c) Field Museum, "Griffin Halls of Evolving Planet," 2006.

DNA Knows Once You Say It, You Can't Take It Back

The diseases in the poem are ones that CRISPR could eradicate because they are caused by mutations in single base pairs or stuck in repetitions—as opposed to diseases caused by numerous factors, including environmental factors and multiple genetic mutations.

One such disease that could be remedied by CRISPR is Huntington disease because the mutation that causes the disease is a repetition of three nucleotides: CAG. "People with Huntington disease have 36 to more than 120 CAG repeats. People with 36 to 39 CAG repeats may or may not develop the signs and symptoms of Huntington disease, while people with 40 or more repeats almost always develop the disorder." From NIH's website U.S. National Library of Medicine: https://ghr.nlm.nih.gov/condition/huntington-disease

The epigraph for the poem is used with permission from the following source:
yourgenome, (2014). November 13, 2014. [online] Available at: https://www.yourgenome.org/facts/what-is-a-genetic-disorder [Accessed 19 February 2015].

What DNA Knows
DNA replication is one of the most basic processes that occurs within a cell. The poem echoes the three steps to replication with the words "initiation, elongation, termination." Another important "three" in the genetic process is that three nucleotides code for every one amino acid, hence the tercets.

A. Experiments with CRISPR On Herself
CRISPR is a new, revolutionary technique that allows scientists with unprecedented accuracy to target and permanently alter the DNA of humans, other animals, and plants for all future generations. It is also relatively cheap to use.

With the rapid development of CRISPR, some people with deadly genetic diseases are presenting themselves as researchers and patients so that they can be a part of the experimental treatments.

DNA "is to": A Quiz
Answer key: **1.** B.; **2.** A. The arrangement of the letters or bases, not the bases or letters themselves, is what makes them significant and become something else; **3.** B. ATCG are the bases (or building blocks) of DNA; **4.** C. The job of the ribosome is to read the mRNA and assemble it into a protein; **5.** A. Proteins act as the basic building blocks to the body; **6.** B. DNA serves more like a record, but RNA represents a living representation of the record; **7.** C. **8.** D.

DNA Offers some Palindromes on the Patent of CRISPR
CRISPR stands for Clustered Interspaced Palindromic Repeats. This poem uses palindromes in every other line.

T. at the Limits of the Possible
The epigraph for the poem is used with permission from the following source:
Clottes, Jean. *What Is Paleolithic Art?: Cave Paintings and the Dawn of Human Creativity.* University of Chicago Press, 2016.

Stubby Horses and Why We Paint Them: An Essay
The anecdote about High Tail in this essay is from the article
"The Secret Lives of Horses" by Wendy Williams, published
in *Scientific American* in October 2015. We are grateful for
permission to use the work, which was adapted from *The Horse:
The Epic History of Our Noble Companion*, by Wendy Williams,
by arrangement with Scientific American/Farrar, Straus and
Giroux, LLC (US), HarperCollins (Canada), Oneworld (UK).
Copyright © 2015 by Wendy Williams.

The essay also quotes from Jean Clottes and is used with
permission from the following source:
Clottes, Jean. *What Is Paleolithic Art?: Cave Paintings and the Dawn
of Human Creativity*. University of Chicago Press, 2016.

**A Pantoum from the Headline: "Y-Chromosomal Adam and
Mitochondrial Eve Never Met"**
Y-chromosomal Adam and Mitochondrial Eve are theoretically
everyone's most common patrilineal and matrilineal ancestors.
Recent studies suggest that they need not have lived at the same
time.

How to Measure Distance
Italics indicate lines are quoted from NASA's Goddard Space
Flight Center website written by Jonathan Keohane and used with
his permission.

Mourning Chicago
The quote in the penultimate stanza is from Ta-Nehisi Coates
Between the World and Me.

Epigraphs from *The Gene: An Intimate History*, by Siddhartha
Mukherjee, copyright 2016 by Siddhartha Mukherjee, MD, are
quoted by permission of Scribner, a Division of Simon & Schuster,
Inc.

Acknowledgements

Grateful acknowledgments to the publications and their editors in which the following poems first appeared. Some of the titles have been changed from their original publication title.

"T. Writes a Letter to A.," "T. Leaves the Doctor's Office," and "Love Between Parents" *Asheville Poetry Review*

"Orderly" and "A. Waits for More Lab Results", which first appeared as "Heredity" *Birmingham Poetry Review*

"A Swim Stroke in Verse: Seventeen Giant Manta Rays and One Hut" *Booth*

"Little U.'s DNA Speaks" first appeared as "Consciousness" *Brevity*

"A., the New Mother, Wants More Instructions" *Bridge Eight*

"A Pantoum from the Headline: Y-Chromosomal Adam and Mitochondrial Eve Never Met" *Connotation Press: An Online Artifact*

"DNA 'is to': A Quiz" *Diagram*

"The Weight of the Sun" *Guernica*

"If It Ever Leaves, Where Does It Go?" *Gulf Coast: A Journal of Literature and Fine Arts*

"How to Measure Distance" *Harvard Review*

"DNA Cautions About Editing the Germline" and "What DNA Knows" *Hopkins Review*

"Helen of Troy" *New Millennium Writings*

"A. Measures Her Child in the Hallway", which first appeared as "A Mother Considers Cell Division" *Nimrod International*

"Black Silhouettes Against a Pink Sunset" *Panhandler Magazine*

"Lightening" *Pleiades*

"After the Last Prognosis," "Attractions," and "While Reading About Semiotics" *Prairie Schooner*

"Zwerp" *Quiddity*

"Among the Yellows" and "I'm Thinking Again of That Lone Boxer" *Rattle*

"DNA's Main Role is the Long-Term Storage of Information" *Shenandoah*

"Joy Is Earned" *The Southern Review*
"Sometimes When a Child Smiles" *Spoon River Poetry Review*
"To Muck and Muck and Muck" *Sweatpants and Coffee*
"Some Madness There" *Tusculum Review*
"Stubby Horses and Why We Paint Them: An Essay" *Zone 3*

And the following anthologies:
"How to Measure Distance" in *Borderlands & Crossroads: Writing the Motherland*
"Mourning Chicago" and "Nightly Call to my Daughter While Traveling" plus reprints of "The Weight of the Sun," "Love Between Parents," "I'm Thinking Again of That Lone Boxer," "Sometimes When a Child Smiles," and "How to Measure Distance" *Journal of the Motherhood Initiative for Research and Community Involvement*

I also want to express my gratitude to David Pruskin and his family for the poems and epigraphs written by Shira Shaiman. Her poems include:
"Cell"
Section two of "Breathing Lessons"
"Anonymous"
"Summer in Dorothy's Garden"
The following quote from "Tender Break" for section three's epigraph:

> *But sunlight was silent*
> *streaming between trees.*
>
> I've failed you,
> *Mother's eyes seemed to say,*
>
> don't become like me.

No book is written without the help of many people. My husband, Adam Prince, is my first and last reader on every poem before I send it out to the world. I'm forever grateful for what he cuts from my poems and for what he adds to my life.

Finally, I want to thank the sun that wakes me, the energy that flows through distribution lines to power my house, the farmers who grow the wheat for my toast, the people I don't know who test my water, the cracking pipes that carry it into my home, the walnut desk that holds me and my micro-circuitry, the 96 million cells I lose per minute and the 96 million cells that replace them, the trees that give their pulp for my paper, and the birds that mumble in the bushes while I type beside them.

Charlotte Pence's first book of poems, *Many Small Fires* (Black Lawrence Press, 2015), received an INDIEFAB Book of the Year Award from Foreword Reviews. She is also the author of two award-winning poetry chapbooks and the editor of *The Poetics of American Song Lyrics*. Her poetry, fiction, and creative nonfiction have recently been published in *Harvard Review*, *Sewanee Review*, *Southern Review*, and *Brevity*. A graduate of Emerson College (MFA) and the University of Tennessee (PhD), she is now the director of the Stokes Center for Creative Writing at University of South Alabama.

9 7 8 1 6 2 5 5 7 1 3 1 1